THE ILLUSTRATED HISTORY OF

CARDIFF'S PUBS

THE ILLUSTRATED HISTORY OF

CARDIFF'S PUBS

Brian Lee

Dedication

In memory of Billy Lee and his
drinking companions.

First published in Great Britain in 2004 by
The Breedon Books Publishing Company Limited
Breedon House, 3 The Parker Centre,
Derby, DE21 4SZ.

This edition published in Great Britain in 2012 by The Derby Books Publishing Company
Limited, 3 The Parker Centre, Derby, DE21 4SZ.

First published 2004, reprinted 2006 & 2012.

ISBN 978-1-78091-181-6

Printed and bound by Copytech (UK) Limited, Peterborough.

CONTENTS

'There is nothing which has
yet been contrived by man,
by which so much happiness
is produced, as by a tavern or
inn.'

Dr Samuel Johnson

Acknowledgements

First of all, I would like to thank my wife Jacqueline who acted as my chauffeuse driving me to many of the pubs featured in this book and to the people who kindly loaned me their photographs. I would also like to thank Clive Williams for writing the foreword. I also need to thank the staff of the Central Library local studies department for their continuing help over the years.

Others I need to thank are the editors of the *South Wales Echo* and the *Cardiff Advertiser* for publishing my requests for photographs in their papers.

My appreciation also to Dennis Pope of Popes Photographic Services who supplied me with many of the photographs. For the loan of other photographs, I am greatly indebted to the following: David Davies FRICS of Stephenson & Alexander, Ken Connelly, John Smith, John Sennett, Harry Welchman, Val Croot, Phylis Shergold, Alun Williams, Ron Humphries, Thelma Davies, Pat Fishlock, Ray Impney, Fred and Maureen MacCormac, Russell Harvey, Toni Jones, Mr & Mrs Don Ross, Colin Duggan, Beryl Harvey, Alan Hambly, Steve Loughlan, John Meazey and David Matthews. I also apologise if I have inadvertently omitted anyone from these acknowledgements.

Brian Lee

FOREWORD

I HAVE known Brian Lee for over 40 years, and was delighted when he asked me to write this foreword to his latest historical offering about his much-loved Cardiff. We have a lot in common. We are former athletes – Brian was a Roath (Cardiff) Harrier and I was with their arch rivals Birchgrove (Cardiff) Harriers. The clubs merged in November 1968 to form Cardiff AAC. But more importantly, we have a deep-seated passion for historical data in general, and as I have been involved in the brewing industry for 43 years, and am still going strong, Brian immediately thought of me to contribute to this fine book.

I have clear recollections of many of Cardiff's pubs – only from a professional standpoint you understand! Gone are the city centre pubs I remember like the Royal Oak, Blue Anchor, Criterion, Queens Head, Blue Bell, Terminus, Great Western and the Royal. All have now been replaced with such evocative establishments as La Brasserie, Champers, Sam's Bar, O'Neills, Goat Major and Old Monk. The Old Monk used to be the Great Western Hotel, which was used as the headquarters of the organising committee for the 1958 Cardiff Empire Games. This building was also used at various times as offices for Welsh Brewers. But are these establishments still pubs, I ask myself? We also have new pubs such as Wetherspoons (three in the city centre at the last count), Walkabout, Bar Med, the Square, and Toad, to name just a few. Again, I ask myself, are these pubs? If they are, they are vastly different from the fine old establishments vividly described in this excellent publication. Many more pubs have disappeared over the years, and Brian recalls lots of these.

One pub in particular that has disappeared has fond memories for me – the Criterion in Church Street. During the early 1960s, it was run at different times by former boxers, Feeny John and Dennis Reardon. Reardon won a boxing gold medal in the 1938 Empire Games in Sydney. I was also very interested to learn that this pub was first called the Shoulder of Mutton, where the famous 19th-century pedestrian William Gale's exploits were planned.

Pubs have to be supplied with beer, and in bygone days, most pubs brewed their own. But, as in other towns and cities, some Cardiff pubs brewed too much for their own use and started to supply other local pubs. This saw the birth of many of the breweries that traded in the city during the last century. At one time there were as many as 100 small breweries of varying sizes in Cardiff and its environs. All except one are no longer with us, either closed without trace or merged, and merged again, to form some of the better-known breweries of the recent past.

Just over 40 years ago, many Cardiffians will remember that the city had four major breweries – Brains, Hancocks, Ely and Crosswells, all of whom supplied the whole of South Wales as well as Cardiff. Indeed no book about Cardiff pubs could be written without mention of the unique contribution made to the city by Brains.

Thankfully, Brains are still going strong, but alas the others are no more. However, in a strange twist, Brains are now brewing in the old Hancocks Brewery in Crawshay Street, just outside the city centre. Their famous Old Brewery in St Mary Street has been redeveloped into a multi-million pound retail development called the Brewery Quarter. The development includes the Albert pub, a famous city centre landmark for generations of rugby fans, which occupied one of the corners of the entrance to the Old Brewery. Brains have a rich and famous heritage and there is no question that their name is synonymous with Cardiff... and hangovers after rugby internationals!

In 1882, the Old Brewery in the heart of Cardiff's city centre was purchased by Samuel Arthur Brain – so that's where S.A. comes from. I thought it stood for Skull Attack! – and his uncle Joseph Benjamin Brain. The company has remained in family ownership ever since and the present chairman, Christopher Brain, is a direct descendant of the founders. Brains purchased South Wales's other leading independent brewer Crown Buckley, of Pontyclun, in 1997, and moved to Crawshay Street in 1999. The company now operates around 220 pubs, mostly in Cardiff and the rest of South Wales, although they also own pubs in the Midlands and West Country.

I have fond memories of the Ely and Crosswells breweries in Ely and Fairwater, where I started work in 1961. Both were part of Rhymney Breweries Ltd, which was formed in May 1959. Rhymney acquired Ely in October of the same year, but Ely ceased brewing in June 1962, and the brewery was demolished the following year. Rhymney Breweries were taken over by Whitbread in 1966 and the company became known as Whitbread Wales in 1969 after Whitbread took over Evan Evans Bevan of Neath.

Many Cardiffians will remember the two breweries straddling the railway line between Ely and Fairwater, close to the Red Lion pub and the old Ely Station. The Red Lion, the brewery 'tap' for so many employees of the two breweries (now renamed the Coach House) stood smack in the middle of both breweries. The Crosswells Brewery stood on the Fairwater side. Confusingly the brewery became known as the 'Ely' brewery following the demolition of the Ely Brewery. The 'Ely' Brewery then became Whitbread's Cardiff brewery and it continued brewing until 1976 when Whitbread moved its brewing activities to their new Magor Brewery on the outskirts of Newport.

Hancocks (along with Fernvale Brewery, Pontygwaith and Webbs of Aberbeeg) became part of the Bass empire in 1968 and traded in Wales as Welsh Brewers. The Brewery in Crawshay Street was built in 1889 by F.S. Lock and bought by Hancocks in 1894. Bass had no further use for the Crawshay Street Brewery following the sale of its brewing interests in 1997, firstly to Belgium's Interbrew, and then to American brewer Coors. So Brains bought it. Most of the Welsh brewers, or Hancocks pubs in Cardiff were sold off, mainly to Punch Taverns, who took over the entire UK stock of about 1,400 Bass leased and tenanted pubs in 1996. Most of the managed pubs remained as part of Six Continents plc until this company itself reorganised in 2003. The pubs are now being operated by Mitchell's and Butlers, an old trading name from the distant Bass past. The other part of the former Six Continents, the hotel company which owns and runs the Holiday Inn chain, has three hotels in Cardiff and now trades as Inter Continental Hotels.

There has been a massive change within the UK brewing industry since the 1989 Beer Orders, and this has resulted in the change of ownership and closure of many popular watering holes in Cardiff and elsewhere. Many pubs are now owned by one of the new pub companies formed in the wake of the Orders. This legislation made the then six national brewers sell off large numbers of their pubs, supposedly to increase choice for consumers. Many believe that the changes have had the reverse effect. So, gone are the pubs previously owned by Hancocks, Ely, and Crosswells, now replaced by pub companies such as Enterprise Inns, Punch Taverns, Innspired Pub Company, Unique Pub Company, Spirit, Heritage Inns and Pubmaster to name a few. Indeed the last named has just been taken over by Punch. Enterprise also own a sizeable chunk of Unique, making Punch and Enterprise the owners of about a quarter of the pubs in the UK. And so the merry-go-round of pub ownership in the UK – and Cardiff continues.

As we have seen, only Brains are left of Cardiff's major brewers, and long may they continue to be independent. Where would Cardiff be without Brains!

Clive Williams, January 2004

INTRODUCTION

SAM ALLEN, in his *Cardiff Reminiscences*, published in 1918, informs us that the town 'had too many public houses and that doing away with a large number of them has been to the advantage of the citizens in general'.

In the central area alone between 1850–75 there were some 93 licenced premises. Then there were the shebeens (illegal drinking dens) where the front rooms of little terraced houses were used for the sale of alcohol.

However, Cardiffians had been wetting their whistles long before then. The burgesses of Cardiff back in 1340 had appointed two ale-tasters, whose job it was to keep a check on the quality and price of the local brew. They did this by sitting on a bench wearing leather trousers which were soaked in ale. If the trousers stuck fast then the ale was deemed fit for consumption.

One of the oldest inn sites is occupied by the Owain Glyndwr in Church Street in the centre of the city. Known as the Mably Arms in 1731, it has since been known as the Kemys Tynte Arms, the Tennis Court and the Buccaneer, before becoming the Owain Glyndwr in the 1970s.

Custom House Street was, from 1800 to around 1872, known as Whitmore Lane. The buildings there were nearly all taverns and many of them had communicating passages into Charlotte Street, which was also full of drinking dens. These taverns were given names that would attract the many sailors on their return from a long sea voyage. For instance, there were the Jolly Boatman, Sailor's Return, Six Bells and Noah's Ark to name just a few.

In 1862, by way of providing a counter-attraction, the town council installed a water fountain in the lane so that the sailors could quench their thirst without having to enter any of these rough and ready public houses. A sign was placed on the fountain which read:

'Stop, seaman, stop and take a draught,

There's danger here both fore and aft,
And learn to shun that wicked craft
who looks at yonder door.

The compass that is stationed here
Will from danger keep you clear
And show you rightly how to steer.
On this dreadful shore,

Heed not the music nor the sport you
Hear in alley, street or court,
They both entice you to a port.
Beset with rock and reef

And ere from then you can return
They'll overhaul the cash you earn
Using you from stern to stern
And bring you all to grief.'

Unfortunately, the sign, along with the drinking cup and chains, was stolen after just a few weeks and never recovered. Charlotte Street was known as 'The Street of Taverns' as it had 12 pubs as well as a porter stores.

Evening Express

Cochfarf was the *nom de plume* of a columnist who used to write for the *Evening Express* at the turn of the century. The following is an extract from his column, which appeared on 8 October 1901 under the heading 'Comments and Criticisms'.

When I was engaged in the building trade it frequently happened that my work mates and I were called upon to deal with strangely-formed houses, which we were informed were once ale-houses, but were closed at the passing of Bruce's Act (about 1868) when houses under a certain assessment were disqualified for licences.

For instance, a house that is occupied to this day at the corner of South and West Church Street was once known as the 'Blacksmiths Arms'. When the owners of these houses desired to retain the licence, a sufficient addition to the premises was ordered to raise the assessments to the qualifying value.

This was the time when the modest Blank Arms became the pretentious Something Hotel. In Cardiff the Carpenters Arms, in the Hayes, became the Oxford Hotel, the Green Dragon, St John's Square became known as Fulton and Dunlop, and the Queen's Head became known as what? Well, Carey's to be sure. Not long ago The Shakespeare cast off its more primitive name and the Cardiff Cottage made room for the King.

The Seven Stars has ceased to shine in Bridge Street; the Six Bells have become silent for ever in Charlotte Street, and the Lakes of Erin have become dry, very dry, in Mary Ann Street. This is about the full extent of my knowledge of Cardiff's older hostelries, but I invite readers to add their information to mine, and thus help the future historians of Cardiff's ale and public houses.

The next day, the following letter appeared in the paper from Mr Charles Evans, of Canton, Cardiff, under the heading:

Vanishing Cardiff
Hostel Names of the Past

Sir,

At the invitation of 'Cochfarf' I will, as far as I am able, add a little of my own knowledge to his of the old hostelries of Cardiff. It is a very interesting subject, because nothing tends to bind the past history of a place with the present as the old hostelries and coffee houses thereof. Here may the young of each succeeding generation foregather and listen to the wonderful stories told by 'old stagers' of the past. Ben Johnson once said that the chief joy of his life was to be in a cosy room of a well conducted hostelry with a few genial companions exchanging views over a pipe (churchwarden) and a glass. 'Cochfarf' must know that Cardiff still possesses a few such houses even now, chief among them being the Globe. What I shall add will be just a word or two about each of the old pubs that I remember as a boy, but which I suppose, 'Cochfarf' has no knowledge of. We will, figuratively speaking, come out of the Globe and enter Womanby Street. The first pub we see, The Horse and Groom, has changed its face but not its name; the next house used to be a very noted hostelry, called the Red Cow. It was, a few years ago, greatly enlarged, going right back to what is now Westgate Street. Its name is altered to the more pretentious one of The Grand. A little lower down the street or lane – Red Cow lane, it was often or not called in the old days – used to be the important and well known Cardiff Boat hostelry kept by my grandfather, Mr David Evans, who was head constable of the town, as his tombstone, now lying at the foot of the Cross in St John's Churchyard, Cardiff, will testify. The house is now practically in ruins, and the licence removed to the Royal Tudor, Tudor Road.

I could dwell a long time here but must hurry along. The next house is the Old Market Tavern, which has been enlarged from the little house it used to be. The next house, which has been abolished a number of years, was called the Butchers' Arms. It stood just where Mrs Barton's, the pork butcher's shop, is. It was at one time kept by an uncle of mine, Mr Henry Martin, who was also a butcher, and whose son, Mr

John Martin, is at present time landlord of the Old Arcade hostelry in Church Street. At the top of the Guildhall, which used to be a very curious house, in as much as the left side of the house was used as a butcher's shop and the right side as the hostel, the kitchen which contained a fireplace that would delight the heart of the coal dealer of today – it was so large; and the settles, high-backed ones, were so comfortable looking. The older butchers of the town will remember George Geffries, the landlord. I will go through some other streets in another letter, and note the changes.

Letter 2

11 October 1901

In 'Cochfarf's' first note he said that the Queen's Head in Queen Street was now familiarly 'known as Carey's' – Alderman Carey's, of course, I may say that before it became the Queen's Head it was a comparatively small house and called the New Inn, whose last landlord was Mr William James. Immediately opposite, on the site of Messrs Rendall's drapery shop, used to be the Unicorn, kept for the last time by Mr John Williams. This house was a favourite resort of the folks from the hills, just as the Mason's Arms, a door or two away was and is to this day, and always will be while the old house stands, so strong is the liking of strangers for one particular 'pub' in any place that they are in the habit of visiting from time to time. They generally bring their families with them, so that their children when they grow up follow suit.

In 'Cochfarf's' note in tonight's *Express* an old Cardiff inhabitant says that the Cardiff Arms is now the Angel. This is not quite correct. 'Tis true that the new Angel stands on a site that was at one time the garden of the Cardiff Arms. The present Angel, which has been built now about nineteen years, is the perpetuation of the old Angel, which was situated where the Bute Estate offices are, in what was those days called Angel Street, but now Castle Street.

Again, 'Old Inhabitant' alludes to the Great Eastern Hotel, Custom House Street. When that little house – very little, indeed – existed, what is now called Custom House Street was then Whitmore Lane. This little house was kept for the last time by my younger brother's father-in-law, and when the corporation wisely decided to do away with all the ramshackle, frowsy, tumble-down hotbeds of sin and iniquity, the licence of this little house was transferred to the Mackintosh Hotel, Cathays. Here also in the lane was the most noted house, and kept by one of the most noted characters in Cardiff – I mean the Flying Eagle 'pub' and its landlord, Jack Matthews. Why a book would hardly contain all that could be told of the Flying Eagle and its landlord, both of whom have gone the way of all men and things these many years. I have dealt with the couple of slight errors or lapses of 'Cochfarf' and 'Old Inhabitant' so I will now begin to tell you what I should have begun to tell at the beginning had it not been for the above-named cause. I intend to take each street in the heart of old Cardiff proper, and name the old 'pubs', that are extinct and those still left, only with changed names. I will start in the lower end of Castle Street and go right up to the Taff Station. The lower end of Castle Street was Broad Street. In this street stood the Cardiff Arms, the Five Bells, the White Lion, and the Cowbridge Arms. The Cardiff Arms upon the East Moors perpetuates this house, but there is a vast difference in both the house and trade of each. The old Cardiff Arms was a very large hotel, with accommodation for a King, if required. The Five Bells was a corner house, standing within the boundary wall of the castle, just to the left of the tower. There was also a court of about a dozen houses alongside the 'pub' which was called Five Bells Court. The White Lion stood immediately in front of the tower – in fact, the clock tower occupied in part the site of the stables of The White Lion. The Cowbridge Arms stood at the end of a row of houses that ran right up to the centre of Castle Street, thus making two streets Angel Street and Castle Street. In Angel Street there were four 'pubs' – the Globe, Ty Dderwyn Deg, the Angel, the Myrtle Tree and the Castle – the last two being next door to each other and right opposite the Angel, the Dderyn Deg (or the Fair Oak of Old Inhabitant) being a little lower down, opposite Hibbert, the seedsman's. We are clear of Castle Street now, and will go further tonight.

Letter 3

14 October 1901

I notice in 'Cochfarf's' notes tonight that Alderman David Jones JP, a genuine old Cardiffian, desires information about a couple of old Cardiff hostelries. It is a strange thing that, although one of them – the Garrick – has only, comparatively speaking, recently assumed that name, yet I for the moment cannot recollect its old name, but I will find out. In regard to the Northumberland Bridge, that was in existence before my time, but I am given to understand that a licenced house used to be just where Messrs Cross's (the ironmongers) place is. It was kept by a Mr Bedlington, and most likely that was it. When I come to deal with St Mary Street I shall name the houses and locate them and they are pretty numerous, I can assure you.

I will now proceed up Duke Street, but before we do so we will go right up to the Castle entrance gate and there by cheek by jowl with the entrance stood a little inn called the Griffins Head kept by John Todd. Now we are in Duke Street the first hostel is of interest to me in as much as a uncle of mine, John Evans, kept it. It was situated just about where Mr Jones the printer is. The next house was situated just about where Mr Marments shop is. It was called the Hope and Anchor and was kept by our justly celebrated local artist Mr Alexander Wilson. The next house was opposite the Old Green Dragon. The New Green Dragon or its more familiar name Fultons takes its place next door. All these houses are now gone. The Glove and Shears still exists also the Rummer Tavern which used to be kept by a rather portly old gentleman named Hopkins who was a member of the good old Cardiff Cricket Club. He was a good bowler, scarcely ever missed a evening's practice during the season. He was very strict in the management of the house. At the bar no one should have more than one drink and as for un-Parliamentary language he utterly abhorred it.

This house was a favourite resort of the local solons. Then we have the Hope and Anchor in Wharton Street. We now enter Smith Street. I must here explain a little. Years ago a row of houses ran right up the middle of Queen Street. Beyond, up as far as the Taff Station, was called Crockherbtown. In Smith Street, just about where the shop of Messrs John Williams & Son is, there stood the Three Cranes hostelry, but it is now extinct as the dodo. I have already alluded to both the old Mason's Arms, which still exists, and also to the Unicorn, which is also extinct. In Queen Street there were no more until we come to the New Inn, now Carey's. I have spoken of this before, so no need to say more now. 'Cochfarf' has spoken about the Crosskeys, on the corner of the Tunnel, being now called the Tivoli. That change is very recent. The next hotel is the Victoria of today, but the London Tavern of years ago; and if I am not mistaken, the (innocent) first cause of these remarks on the subject, was the person responsible for the change in the name of this house, namely Mr Councillor Gerhold, who for some years was the proprietor of it. You see, Sir, his constitutional principles as his loyalty bubbles over even in the names of his houses – from the Cottage to The King, and from the Tavern to Victoria.

A little further up Crockherbtown, on the right-hand side, as far as Mr Soloman Andrews's shop, in the old days just about there stood the most picturesque little pub of the town. You went down three steps off the pavement to enter this little house, a strip of garden ran the length of it, and it was straw thatched, hence its name, the Thatched House Tavern, kept by Mr Herbert Rees who, like another landlord of his time Mr Fred Armstrong, of the Dderwyn Ddeg, was very partial to white hats. There is just one more up here, and that is the Alexandra. It is greatly enlarged and altered. Its former name was Winstones, being kept by the late Alderman John Winstone, a rare old bluff gentleman, who for some years like a good many more bonifaces, was a member of our local parliament.

The Boar's Head (Church Street) was just about where Mr Bayles boot shop is now. Standing in Broad Street I follow the names given – Cardiff Arms, Five Bells, White Lion, Cowbridge Arms, and in Angel Street Ty-Dderwyn Ddeg, Angel Hotel, Maple Tree and Castle. But I think when a errand boy in Mitchell's boot and shoe shop at the top end of Angel Street right opposite High Corner House making the entrance to the Castle gate coming from St Mary Street, and at the end of Castle Street, facing the Bank of Mitchell's premises there was a pub its back running right to the Castle's gate.

Letter 4

17 October 1901

I forgot to speak of St John's Square or, as it was called in olden times, St John Street. Right up to the centre of the street, or square, as it exists today, there was a row of small houses, just as in Castle Street and Queen Street. On the left side entering from Queen Street and just where the fishmonger Mr Good's shop is or else where the six and a half pence bazaar is there was a little hostel called the Lamb. It no longer exists, although in Canton we have a Lamb and Flag.

A little lower down where the Bombay tea shop is there was another inn called the Brown Bear kept by Stanley the Hatter. 'Cochfarf' has already alluded to the New Green Dragon (Fultons and Little Nells) of today but Tennis Court of old. In those days it was no uncommon thing to see a parson and congregation, or some of them, engaged in a game of wall tennis. Often the parson's house end would constitute the tennis court. It must not be forgotten that St John's vicarage was in the old days within the precincts of the present boundary's rulings, so that anyone can understand how it is that the Tennis Court hostel was and is in close proximity to the parson's house and church.

Now we will go down High Street and the Parish. As I said before in locating and naming the old hostelries we are bound to be more or less geographical. I therefore am bound to tell those of you who do not know that right up the middle of High Street (not all the way) there ran a block of buildings, chief among them being the Town Hall. This block commenced opposite what is now Lipton's Shop but what in the old days was a little inn called the Wheatsheaf, together with the Wheatsheaf which used to be on part of the ground taken up by Howells in Trinity Street. The Wheatsheaf in High Street was at the beginning of a sort of arcade that led to the old meat market whose outlet was by the Three Tuns in Duke Street.

There were no more on that side of High Street but on the other side there was the Blue Bell and Three Horse Shoes which are just the same now as ever with the exception of a little alteration. One house has been done away with, the Sugar Loaf, which was situated as nigh as possible to Dale, Forty & Co. the piano makers. The Guildhall, which has an outlet or inlet into Quay Street, used to be called The Griffin.

Almost immediately opposite was a little pub kept by Mrs Bedlington (can't think of name). A little further on the opposite side is the Bodega of today but the Borough Arms of old. Now this was a noted house and here would foregather all the local prophets and oracles and what wonder seeing that its landlord, Mr William Davies, was also the borough treasurer and he could tell a thing or two how the town stood in a financial, social or religious sense, because it was known that he was at the same time in public and sat at the receipt of custom, also superintendent of St John's Sunday Schools.

He was a great enthusiast in kite flying. He used to make peculiar kites in the form of birds. When the children's Whitsun Treat came off he generally attended with his kites for their amusement. He believed in Sunday closing long before the operating of the Sunday Closing Act. The Garrick of today was the Clarence of a few years ago but in the days of yore it was called the Sunderland Bridge and was kept by James Howells. In passing, I may say that alongside this house, the entrance into Morgan's Arcade, Mr Tim Donovan, of 'Maid of Killarney' fame, kept a marine store, whilst his wife looked after a little shop just above the store. Now Mrs Donovan was truly and justly accorded the stoutest and heaviest woman in Cardiff or for miles around it. It is related of her that after a great difficulty she managed to get into a cab, which she had no sooner done than crash went the cab, and to extricate her from the wreck was a more difficult task than to get her in. [Author's note: A well-known rag and bone man, Tim Donovan and his mare Maid of Killarney once won a steeplechase at Cowbridge Races after racing everything on the roads to the racetrack. A whimsical Irishman, he bought the mare for 25 shillings and a pint and won many horse jumping prizes with her at Sophia Gardens Horse Show.] The next house was situated a couple of doors down above where Messrs Morgan's shop is; it is not now in existence. It was called the Royal George. 'Cochfarf' has already alluded to the old Carpenters' Arms, now the Oxford. Years ago on the ground that the Batchelor monument and the underground public convenience occupies there was a block of buildings, commencing with a single house just where the statue is. This house was a corner-house-in-the-middle of the street sort-o-house – well, to be strictly accurate it was in the middle of The Hayes, and was noted for its excellent sausages and baked faggots, either hot or cold. You must, Mr Editor, please excuse me for going off the track of the pubs to the faggot shop. There is nothing in the world that quickens one's memory so quickly as the sense of smell and in fancy I can see the piping hot faggots, and, as Dan Leno would say, 'hear the lovely smell of Billy Ayers' baked faggots'. This block of buildings extended and widened as it exists, up to about where the road is in front of the free library buildings, one side forming a continuation of Working Street, and the other, if I remember rightly, called Victoria Place. It really was a continuation of Trinity Street. On the Working Street side of this block there were no pubs and on the Trinity Street side there was only one, and that is there today, namely the Rising Sun.

On the side of the library and museum there used to be a chapel, a pub, a court, cottages, and a row of other cottages and business houses on the Trinity Street side. On the Trinity Street or south-west corner the pub was situated. It was called the Royal Hotel. It was kept for the last time by Mrs Burns, who together with the licence, went to the Royal George at the upper end of Castle Road. The name of the court was Winstones. I forget what religious body the chapel belonged to. The next house will be the last, and that was kept by Jimmy Holland the Cardiff jockey. It was called the Black or the White Horse, and used to be where Fultons house is now or very near to it.

Under the heading 'More Reminiscences' the following letter appeared under the above letter.

Sir,
The discussion about the 'old pubs' of Cardiff is interesting to both the old residents, as reviving old memories, and to those who have resided here only, say, since about 25 or 26 years, when the borough was

expanded at a bound by the inclusion of Roath and Canton within its boundaries. For some years after the opening of the West Bute Dock (in 1839), there was no semblence of a town lower than St Mary's Church (which was opened in 1843), so the seafaring people flocked to the upper part of the present town, notably to St Mary Street and places north of the Junction Canal.

About the period of the forties up to the fifties, the most notable rendezvous of captains and sailors were the Bute Arms, then kept by Mr William Taylor (father of Dr William Taylor), Royal Oak, the present Garrick was the Sunderland Bridge (not Northumberland), kept by James Howells (who subsequently built the present Hastings Hotel – 'on a pool of mud', as he said to me).

Then, higher up in St Mary Street, the Cottage, kept by Mr Phil Bird; the Black Lion, kept by Mr Charles Samuel Twigg, who undoubtedly had the best patronage of the lot, the captains, especially the Whitehaven traders, thronging his parlours, and the sailors the kitchens and other places in the rear. Further up was the Griffin; the Three Horse Shoes, kept by Mr Watson; the Sugar Loaf, kept by Mr Wood (who subsequently took the Cardiff Arms); then the Blue Bell, kept by Mr Thomas Williams; the Angel Hotel, where the mail coaches all stopped to be re-horsed; the Globe, Mr Christopher French; the Cardiff Arms, Mr Thomas Ainsley; White Lion (right in front of the splendid clock tower of the Castle); Five Bells, kept by Mrs Jane Brown (grandmother of Mr H.O. Fisher).

In Duke Street there was the Three Tuns, the Green Dragon, the Old Green Dragon and the Glove and Shears. In the present St John's Square, the late Mr W.

Nell took in 1846 to the present well known place opposite the church. Right the other side, old Mr William Stanley kept the Bull. At the corner of North and Queen streets, the present Red Lion was reared on the site of one of the oldest buildings in the town, reputed to be 400 years old. It was in a room at the back of the old Red Lion that the few Roman Catholics then residing in Cardiff privily held their services before the Catholic Relief Bill was passed about 1828 or 1829.

Further on there was another old 'pub' the Three Cranes, which has been so beautifully improved out of all recognition as to result in the present elegant and glittering shop of Messrs John Williams & Sons. Further on the present elegant antique Masons Arms still exists; opposite it was the New Inn (the present Alderman Carey's Place). A few yards further on, where the Tivoli now stands, stood the old Cross Keys, a hostelry of which I believe but very few people have a full conception of its curious records. Prior to the incorporation of Cardiff it lay outside the borough, which was bounded by the town wall on the west side of the canal. It was in this house accordingly the Courts Leet of the Barony belonging to the Bute Estate were held, and, indeed continued to be held until very recent times. It is tedious to detail all about the old pubs, although more might easily be dwelt upon, but I may mention another thing, connected though it is, with but a very small place, yet has a strange interest in it. The Earl of Windsor Inn in a little street running from Union Street to Paradise Place was named so shortly after the birth of the late Marquess of Bute, in 1847, and who was then declared Earl of Windsor by his father, and continued so till his father died in March 1848, when of course, the courtesy title elapsed. The above I have jotted down on the run, I can write no more now.

More anon, if you like – I am etc & co J.P. Cathays, 15 October.

Letter 5

21 October 1901

Across the road from the old Borough Arms was the Bath Arms. This stood where the bank is, lower down a door or two was the Rock & Fountain kept by Mr Palfrey. The next house was the Pine Apple two doors below. This house had for its landlord at one time the celebrated pugilist Dan Thomas, one of the most inaffected and pleasant little men alive under normal circumstances but look out for squalls when his back hair was up. The Butchers Arms in Quay Street landlord was Billy Gale, one of the smartest walkers. He performed at Canton many years ago and walked 2,000 quarter miles in 2,000 quarter hours consecutively.

In Wharton Street, in Broth Lane, as the old folk termed it, on the right-hand side is Bakers Row. In the old days before you entered the row proper you had to pass through Ready Money Lane. There were only two small cottages, one of which was occupied by one of Cardiff's odd characters Tom Rosser. As children we used to give the poor old woke sticks, paper, old books etc which he ate. [Author's note: Tom Rosser travelled the streets of Cardiff with his donkey cart selling sand which in those days was used on the floors of houses. He would often stop at a pub and treat his donkey to a pint.]

After passing through this lane we turn right and in the most out of the way place was called The Hole In The Wall, kept by Mr Jones who combined the business of publican with that of a marine store situated about the back of Westminster Stores. This Mr Jones was the father of Henry Jones who sat in the Cardiff Council as one of the Park Ward representatives.

The next house up here was The Golden Lion kept by a lady named Baber. It stood on ground now taken up by James Howell. Returning to St Mary Street we find the Morning Star just about where Messrs Masters & Co. Clothiers Shop as well as the Napier that was about where Mr Perkins the iron mongers is. James Thomas landlord. Next house Theatre Royal old name Talbot Arms. The next abolished house was Ship & Pilot Inn. The last hotel that side, the Terminus, used to be called The Steam Mill Inn. Where the Express office stood was the Old Cornish Mount. I think the Great Western Hotel when it was built had this licence transferred to it. The next house was a little higher up towards the Royal. It was called Stogumber Tavern. A little further up still, just where Mr Brook's the auctioner place is, was a little court of small houses, and the Sloop Inn was placed on the corner of this little court. From the Town Hall down to this little court there were two other courts, namely Landore and Vachell's Court, the entrance to which exactly where the Prudential Offices and Daltons Court, the entrance to which was just about where the talking machine shop is.

Daltons Court contained about ten or twelve nice cottages and was cleanly kept. Vachells Court was, well, Vachells Court. The old vegetable market was held in the middle of St Mary Street out in the open. The crude stalls would be end to end, some built in the manner of costers, as they used to be in the Hayes, only with this difference, that old-time goods of today.

Here in a space underneath the old town hall steps was the poultry and butter market. Almost adjoining the cheese market was a very rough place where the 'boys' who on a Saturday night drank not wisely but were too well immured pending their appearance before the 'beaks' which usually led to the culprits being placed in the stocks that used to be in front of the old town hall. The old workhouse used to be where the water works engineers office is – the late Post Office in St Mary Street – whilst the old gaol was just about where Stedalls mantle shop is. The public shambles were situated in Quay Street and Westgate Street. The Maltsters Arms in North Street or North Road no longer exists. The original name of Carey's was the Prince Regent afterwards New Inn now Queens or Careys.

Letter 6

24 October 1901

In Caroline Street there were so many pubs and so close together that their names are almost forgotten by me. One of them was the Happy Return (landlady Moll Price). At the old Custom House at the bridge end of Custom House Street everything in connection with the shipping of vessels or crews took place and there were any number of little pubs. Charlotte Street, which was at the back of Whitmore Lane (or Custom House Street of today) there were no less than ten or twelve. Here the decoys of the poor sailors – the ladies of easy virtue – resorted and by their wiles led poor Jack into them, and the sequel generally was his departure fleeced of every single dime and often minus the best part of his clothes.

A few houses were honourable exceptions. Custom House Bridge kept by Mrs Richards whose son John was steward of the Conservative Working Men's Club in St Mary Street. The little house in the middle of Caroline Street, The Neptune, was then the same as it is today much interested in finding sturdy young men who were willing to take the Queen's shilling. Kept by Mr Hannen. In The Hayes after leaving Caroline Street the first house the Duke Of Wellington is greatly enlarged from the little house it used to be when Mr Lenord kept it.

The Pavillion of today used to be the Duke Of Cornwall landlord James Nolan. The next house was situated a couple of doors above where Messrs Morgan's shop is. Royal George. Trinity Street site was the Rising Sun. Working Street was kept by Jimmy Holland the Cardiff jockey called the Black or White Lion where Fultons is now.

Letter 7

28 October 1901

Sir, I certainly agree with you that the proposed change of the name of Ye Old Black Lion to the Sandringham or any other would be doing away with a interesting and historical Cardiff sign, and also with old associations still, I trust, remembered by many an old Cardiffian. The ancient hostelry has stood in St Mary Street, and formed in bygone days a close link between the family that bore the arms or crest of the Black Lion and the town of Cardiff. All the older signs of our inns refer to some part of our local history.

Personally, I shall very much regret the change, as my paternal uncle, one Dafydd Rees, of the Black Lion (at one time a well-known Boniface), owned and kept the house for many years. The inn, whilst not being so pretentious as the Angel and the Cardiff Arms (which at the time I write of were the two principal hotels in

Cardiff), was still a public house of the good old fashioned sort, where an excellent ordinary could be obtained and it was a house much loved by the yeomen farmers of Glamorgan and Monmouthshire especially on fair and market days.

The local fairs were then held in the streets of Cardiff, and the old market place occupied a position at the rear of the Town Hall in the centre of High Street. The Old Black Lion was, literally speaking, a house of entertainment for man and beast, and many a Cardiff tradesman of the old school and several old salts of the small port of the River Taff were wont to congregate at the hostelry in the evenings, and to take their ease at that inn.

The following list of pubs is taken from volume five of the *Cardiff Borough Records* published at the beginning of the 20th century.

The Older Inns of Cardiff

Authors of fiction have often revelled in the atmosphere of romance which hangs about an old inn. Even poets have not disdained to sing the charms of an ancient hostelry. Antiquaries are well aware of the interest attaching to inns and inn signs, particularly to heraldic signs.

In those of the Cardiff district the names and arms of the principal local families are represented, and we have examples of most of the quaint titles by which Boniface has in all ages been want to designate his hospitable house. This schedule, however, comprises only the names and signs of inns which may be termed old established, from the palatial hotel down to the humble tavern.

Wherever possible I have mentioned the earliest date at which the name of the inn has been found in records and, in the case of houses which are no longer licensed, the latest date also. The situation of each house is also given, where it could be ascertained.

ALEXANDRA. Crockherbtown (*c.*1875). North-west corner of Taff Vale Approach. An early Victorian house with a porch on the pavement, modernised *c.*1895.

ANGEL. North side of Angel Street (1666, 1731, 1792). A later inn under this sign and the same licence was on the south side of the street, but is now the Bute Estate Office. At the latter transformation the licence was transferred to the Cardiff Arms. When the last named hotel was built it was called the Angel.

BEAR. (1719, 1770).

BELL.

BLACK BEAR. (1798).

BLACK LION. On the east side of Saint Mary Street (1792, 1798).

BLACK LION. Llandaff; south-east corner of High Street and Cardiff Road. The sign is taken from the arms of Mathew of Llandaff, 'Or, a lion rampant sable.'

BLUE ANCHOR. In Saint Mary Street, on the east side, adjoining the new Market (1711, 1792, 1835). Now near the south end of the street.

BLUE BELL. High Street (1873).

BOAR'S HEAD. Somewhere near the Market Tavern (1792, 1835).

BOAR'S HEAD. South-east side of Leckwith Road, Canton Common.

CANTON CROSS. West side of Canton Cross.

CARDIFF ARMS. An important inn which stood in Broad Street, Cardiff, at the west end of Angel Street (1792). It occupied the site of a very ancient building known as the Red House, in Welsh Ty Coch, a name by which the inn was long known (1710, 1731, 1777, 1778). The Cardiff Arms was demolished 1878, in the course of street improvements. Its licence was transferred to a house erected near the old site, but which took the name of The Angel from another discontinued hostelry in

Angel Street (now Castle Street). The Cardiff Arms was so called after this house.

CARDIFF BOAT. Womanby, corner of Quay Street (1792, 1829).

CARDIFF CASTLE. High Street. It was a ruinous house in 1849.

CARDIFF COTTAGE. East side of Saint Mary Street.

CARPENTER'S ARMS. The Hayes, east side.

CASTLE. Angel Street. Sold under the Improvement Act in 1878.

CLIFTON. At the corner of Clifton Street and Broadway, Roath. Also known as the Tredegar Arms. The Roath Local Board met here in 1859.

COCK. On the east side of the North Gate (1731, 1787).

CORNISH ARMS. Charlotte Street (1865).

COW AND SNUFFERS. Llandaff Yard. The sign is said to be the result of a tour-de-force by Lord Beaconsfield, who invented it as the most incongruous title conceivable.

COWBRIDGE ARMS. Broad Street. Sold under the Improvement Act in 1878.

CROSS INN. Cross Street (1868).

CROSS KEYS. On the south side of Queen Street, by the Tunnel just outside the East Gate (1792, 1806). Lord Bute formerly held here his annual Court Leet for the Manor of Roath-Dogfield. In 1896 the name of the house was changed to The Tivoli – as 'more artistic'.

CROW. (1770).

DOLPHIN. 'The Old Dolphin', South side of Church Street. Perhaps identical with the Ship and Dolphin.

DUKE OF WELLINGTON. The Hayes, near Waterloo Buildings.

ESPLANADE. Beach Road, Penarth. This hotel represents the old Penarth Beach Inn, demolished c.1875.

FAIR OAK. Angel Street (1861).

FIVE BELLS. In Broad Street (1748, 1792, 1821). Pulled down c.1859, on the erection of the new bridge over the mill leat.

FOUR ELMS. Elm Street Roath. So called from its proximity to the Four Elms (1859).

FOX AND HOUNDS. Whitchurch.

GENERAL NOTT. The westernmost house of the middle row in Smith Street. The north part of it, which had been the Post Office, was demolished 1849. The other part was occupied latterly by Battista Pedrazzini, watchmaker.

GEORGE. At the West Gate (1710, 1780).

GLOBE. East corner of Castle Street and Homanby (1731).

GLOVE AND SHEARS. Duke Street, at the corner of North Street (1792). The Judges' servants used to be lodged here (1829). The house displays a Welsh announcement: 'Cymry a Chymraeg i mewn' (Welsh people and Welsh speaking within).

GOLDEN LION. Between Saint Mary Street and Barry Lane. The mail-coach horses used to be stabled here. The yard was in the occupation of the South Wales Carriage Co. until 1898, when the Morgan Arcade was built over it. Baker's Row runs southward from Wharton Street to Barry Lane. Before reaching Greenmeadow Court it widened out into Golden Lion Court. The inn stood at the east corner of Wharton Street and Baker's Row.

GOLDEN LION. Glebe Street, Penarth. Starting place of the Cardiff breaks.

GREEN DRAGON, The (New). A former name of Messrs. Fulton & Dunlop's wine and spirits vaults, at the corner of Duke Street and St John Square (1792, 1825).

GREEN DRAGON, The (Old, 1720, 1792).

GREYHOUND (1777, 1792).

GRIFFIN. High Street (1798, 1827).

GRIFFIN. St Mary Street. Sign derived from the arms of the family of Morgan of Tredegar.

GRIFFIN. Lisvane.

HEATHCOCK. High Street (1674).

HEATHCOCK. City of Llandaff. A heathcock is the family crest of Mathew of Llandaff.

HOLE-IN-THE-WALL. Somewhere near the north side of Wharton Street (1848–79). Query whether a corruption of 'Heol-y-cawl'?

HORSE AND GROOM. West side of Womanby.

IRISHMAN'S GLORY. Charlotte Street (c.1830).

IVY BUSH. Corner of St Mary Street and Mill Lane (1867).

JOLLY BOATMAN. Charlotte Street (c.1830).

KEMYS-TYNTE ARMS. Later known as the Tennis Court, now Nell's Brewery and licensed premises, between Church Street and St John Square. This was anciently the town house of the Kemys-Tynte family.

KING DAVID. (1750).

KING'S ARMS. In Castle Street (1833).

KING'S CASTLE. On the north side of the Cowbridge Road, at the south-east corner of King's Road. Named after the King's Castle, an ancient building which stood a short distance further east (1866).

KING'S HEAD. (1719, 1792). St Mary Street, where the Town Hall was erected in 1849. The inn was ordered to be pulled down in 1850.

LAMB. Trinity Street (1818).

LAMB AND FLAG. Next to the King's Head, where the Town Hall was built in 1849, on the west side of Saint Mary Street.

MALTSTER'S ARMS. In the city of Llandaff.

MARKET TAVERN. In Trinity Street (1840). It was originally called the New Market Inn, and had an opening into Church Street.

MASON'S ARMS. On the north side of Queen Street near the East Gate (1792, 1822). It is still standing, though threatened.

MERRY HARRIERS. In the parish of Llandough, at the Cogan crossroads.

MITRE. City of Llandaff. This house was the property of the Dean and Chapter in 1750, when it was rebuilt.

NEW INN. South side of Queen Street, just within the East Gate and the canal. Also called the Prince Regent. Late Carey's spirit vaults. The name occurs in 1768.

OLD ARCADE. A part of this inn is built over the passage from Church Street to the Market, hence the name. This was the first of Cardiff's numerous arcades.

OLD HOSTRY, The. (1600).

PANNIERS. (1596).

PINE APPLE. Whitchurch Road, Llandaff Yard.

PLOUGH AND HARROW. (1792).

PORCUPINE. (1596).

PRINCE REGENT. On the south side of King Street, now Queen Street, just within the East Gate and the canal, opposite the Mason's Arms and the Unicorn (1829). Late Carey's spirit vaults. Also called the New Inn.

QUEEN'S HOTEL. On the west side of St Mary Street, just north of the end of Wharton Street. It was called the Stogumber Hotel in 1861. Rebuilt *c*.1895.

RED COW. Womanby Street (1776, 1792). Uninhabited from about 1890, but still standing in 1903. It was from this house that the Cowbridge carrier used to start.

RED LION. East corner of Smith Street and North Street (1792, 1809). Still licensed, 1903. Mass was for a time said in the ordinary room of this inn, at the beginning of the 19th century.

RISING SUN. On the west side of the Hayes, a little south of Wharton Street, and on the north-east corner of Rising Sun Court. Demolished 1898.

ROCK AND CASTLE. On a rocky eminence behind Pentyrch Church, the site of Pentyrch Castle.

ROSE AND CROWN. On the east side of the North Gate (1787). It still exists.

ROYAL HOTEL. On the west side of St Mary Street, at the north-east corner of Wood Street (1870). Rebuilt *c*.1895.

ROYAL OAK. St Mary Street (1683).

ROYAL OAK. Whitchurch.

RUMMER TAVERN. South side of Duke Street.

SHIP. (1792, 1798).

SHIP AND CASTLE. In High Street, opposite the Wheat Sheaf (1792, 1821).

SHIP AND DOLPHIN. Church Street (1792, 1818).

SHIP ON LAND, Ship on Launch. Quay Street.

SHOULDER OF MUTTON. (1731, 1792, 1812).

STAR. Llanilltern.

SWAN. High Street (1666). The Little Swan, 1731.

TENNIS COURT. An old name (but lately revived) for the licensed premises attached to Nell's Brewery (1731, 1829). It was so called from a tennis court which was made in what is now the yard of the brewery, behind the houses which form the north-east end of Church Street. Before that court was constructed (c.1777), the tennis balls were thrown against the north wall of Saint John's church tower, hard by. A still older name for this house was the Kemeys-Tynte Arms, it having anciently been the townhouse of that family.

THATCHED HOUSE. Lewis Street, west side near the Hayes bridge. This is said to have been the last thatched house in the town.

THREE CASTLES. (1792, 1798).

THREE CRANES. St Mary Street or High Street (1770, 1792, 1842).

THREE CUPS. Llandaff Yard.

THREE ELMS. Whitchurch Green.

THREE HORSE SHOES. High Street, west side (1798).

THREE MARINERS. Near the Quay (1779).

THREE SALMONS. (1793).

THREE TUNS. (1792, 1798).

TON INN, The Old. Tongwynlais.

TY PWLL COCH. Pwll Coch, Ely Common. On the north side of the Cowbridge Road.

UNICORN. North side of Smith Street, now Queen Street, between the East Gate on the east and the Masons' Arms inn on the west (1772, 1829). It stood on the site of the town wall, where now is Herne's draper's shop, close to the canal. It was demolished c.1877.

UNICORN. Llanedern village, close to the church. A comfortable old thatched house, with an inn-kitchen of the

picturesque sort, open chimney, oak settles, and flitches of
bacon under the beams; and a native Welsh-speaking landlady.

WHEAT SHEAF. In High Street, opposite the Ship and Castle
(1821).

WHITE HORSE. (1772).

WHITE LION. In Castle Street (1778, 1798).

WHITE LION. In the hamlet of Ely.

Did You Know?

In the course of the research for this book I have unearthed the
following information about some of Cardiff's older pubs.

OLD SHOULDER OF MUTTON

The Old Shoulder Of Mutton (later the Criterion) in Church
Street was where local sportsmen would meet to arrange
exhibitions of Billy Gale's walking prowess. A celebrated figure in
Cardiff in the 1880s, Billy Gale, a wiry little man, performed
wonderful feats of endurance walking. His first walking exhibition
took place in Canton in 1876 where he walked 1,000 miles inside
1,000 hours.

THE BIRDCAGE INN

The Old Arcade in Church Street was once known as the Birdcage
Inn. The landlord was skilled in making cages for larks and linnets,
which he fashioned in his spare time from old floorboards. The bar
was decorated throughout by these birdcages which he sold to his
patrons. Hence the name of the Birdcage Inn.

FREDERICK STREET PUBS

In days gone by Frederick Street certainly had its share of pubs.
These included the Burnham Inn (1897), Bute Castle Hotel
(1863), Castle Brewery (1855), Manchester Unity Tavern (1858),
Marchioness of Bute Inn (1855), King's Head Tavern (1858), Stag
and Hounds (1897), Ivorites Arms (1855) and Pembroke Castle

Inn. The pubs in Little Frederick Street were the Shamrock and Leek Tavern (1858), Joiners Arms (1858), Dublin Arms (1897) and the Lifeboat (1897).

BUTCHER'S ARMS

In the 1800s, the Butcher's Arms in Whitchurch was the place for those Cardiffians with a sporting interest. The landlord, Mr Isaac Edwards, who was a butcher, staged all sorts of games like quoits, pitching, rounders and foot races. These foot races, usually over 100 or 120 yards, took place on the main road for £5 a side and hundreds would gather to witness the events. The neighbouring Old Three Horse Shoes and Birchgrove inns, not to be outdone, sometimes staged trotting matches and horses used to race on the Caerphilly and Whitchurch roads. On one famous occasion, two local farmers backed their horses for a £100 a side trotting match which was to start at 9am in the morning on Whitchurch Road. But long before that hour vehicles of every description came from far and near and the crowd that assembled along the route was so great that four mounted officials had great difficulty in clearing the course. After some delay, the race got under way and it was Mr Artemus Ward's horse that emerged the winner. A band was soon found and singing and dancing went on long into the night. From that day on the great occasion was known as Trotting Match Day.

LLANRUMNEY HALL

Some historians claim that Llanrumney Hall was the burial place of Llywelyn Llyw Olaf, the last Welsh Prince of Wales. Ancient manuscripts were said to assert that the headless body of Llywelyn was interred at this former monastery, the fine old Elizabethan mansion which once stood in a well wooded park. Apparently, after Llywelyn was killed in a skirmish with some English soldiers near Builth Wells his head was dispatched to King Edward I, who was staying at Conway Castle. However, Llywelyn's headless body was alleged to have been secretly brought by the monks to

Llanrumney Hall, which in those days was known as Little Keynsham, on account of its close association with Keynsham Abbey in Somerset. There was said to be a statement in writing by the granddaughter of a Mr Moggridge, who once owned Llanrumney Hall, to the effect that her grandfather's workmen discovered in the vaults of the hall a stone coffin, placed in a very thick wall of masonry, which contained the remains of Llywelyn Ein Llyw Olaf whose body had never before been discovered. An acknowledged historian Professor Freeman, who once resided in Llanrumney Hall, also believed that the remains were those of the last Welsh Prince of Wales.

THE BLUE BELL

Llanrumney Hall, which is now a public house on the Llanrumney Council estate, was once a monastery and in days long gone the monks, to celebrate St Melo's feast day (22 October), used to organise an annual sports and jollification day. The main event was a foot race from the monastery to St Mellons Church, and the winner received a most unusual prize. His reward was the monastery's sanctus bell, which had a blue clapper. However, he did not keep it for more than a few hours as his prize was really the honour of restoring the bell to its use in the monastery. In later years the finish of the race, for some reason or other, was changed. The runners finished at a spot that is now the site of the Blue Bell Inn, St Mellons, and this is one explanation of how the pub got its name. The Blue Bell was said to have been built chiefly to provide accommodation for the gentry and their horses, who came from different parts of the parish and who attended St Mellons Church.

ROMPNEY CASTLE

The Rompney Castle replaced an earlier inn known as the Pear Tree. It was said that the old inn was built from the stones of a Norman castle. Popular with local farmers and fishermen, it was once the haunt of smugglers that operated from an ancient manor

Ty Mawr that gave its name to nearby Ty Mawr Road. The Pear Tree was bought by the first American Consul to Cardiff who added a mock baronial hall to the building and renamed it Rompney Castle.

THE ANTHONYS
The Anthonys in Ely was named after three famous Welsh jockeys, and built on the site of the old racecourse in the 1960s.

THE DUSTY FORGE
Now a community centre, The Dusty Forge in Ely dated to around 1790.

HIGHFIELDS INN
The haunted Highfields Inn, another well-known Ely watering hole, was once a farmhouse.

THE RED HOUSE
This historic pub in Ferry Road, the only one in Cardiff which had a navigation light, opened in 1871 as a hotel which provided overnight accommodation for sailors. It had a licence to serve 'tea, coffee and intoxicating liquor to the working classes'. Originally known as the Penarth Railway Hotel, it was renamed The Red House in 1926. On one occasion it was painted white but after complaints from regulars it was repainted red. Despite a long-running campaign to save it, this once popular Victorian pub was bulldozed in 2005.

Chapter One
City Centre Pubs

Nineteenth-century St Mary Street. The Pine Apple Inn and the Rock and Fountain can be seen left of picture.

The Pine Apple was established around 1858 and the Rock and Fountain in 1875. Charlotte Palfrey was the licensee of the latter pub in 1885. Both pubs were demolished in 1891.

The British Volunteer on The Hayes, which dated to 1863, had three public rooms. For many years it was run by the Dancer family until it was demolished to make way for the Hayes House shopping complex.

The White Hart Hotel stood on the corner of Little Bridge Street and Bridge Street from 1858 until 1926.

The Masons Arms in Queen Street (earlier Smith Street) was situated where the entrance of Superdrug is today. The postbox in the picture is believed to have been the first one in Cardiff.

This is how The Masons Arms (1795–1920) looked in 1903.

The Cowbridge Arms (1863–1900) stood on the corner of Angel Street and Broad Street. It was situated at the end of a row of houses that ran right in the centre of Castle Street.

On the corner of Kingsway and Queen Street (formerly North Street and Smith Street) stood the Red Lion (1792–1958). Before there were Catholic churches in Cardiff, Mass was celebrated there in the ordinary room.

Left and below: The Three Horse Shoes Inn (1798–1913) was in High Street.

Opposite page: The Borough Arms in St Mary Street was established in 1873. From time to time it has also been called The Bodega.

Right and below: The Globe in Castle Street was established in 1731. It has also been known as Duke's and Four Bars Inn and is reputed to be haunted.

PENINSULA · WATERLOO · SEVASTAPOL · ALI · ASJID · AFGHANISTAN · EGYPT

LONG LIFE TO OUR SOLDIER PRINCE
OF THE GALLANT HUSSARS.

PHIL HARMONIC RESTAURANT & SILVER GRILL

TELEPHONE No.
THE
DONALDSON
BROTHERS

TRUMAN & Cᵒ
LONDON STOUT

ALLSOPP'S
BURTON ALE

Previous page: The Philharmonic in St Mary Street was established in 1887. It was renamed The Harlech Tavern during the 1960s and reverted to its original name in 1978. This picture was taken when the Duke of Clarence visited the town in 1890.

Above and below: Many Cardiffians will remember the Rose and Crown in Kingsway (formerly North Street), which was demolished in 1974 despite a campaign to get it listed by the Welsh Office. A new Rose and Crown was built near the site, but was renamed Coopers in 1997 and later became the Barfly. The earliest record of it is in 1787.

At one time, the Marchioness of Bute in Frederick Street had a brewery adjacent to it. Established in around 1846, it was still serving pints in the 1960s.

The Taff Vale Inn on the corner of Paradise Place and Queen Street had already closed when this picture was taken in 1978.

A feature of the Rummer Tavern in Duke Street is its wood-panelled walls and stone-flagged floors. Dating to 1813, and formerly known as Hallinans, it is said to be haunted.

Established in around 1887, the Park Lane Bar on the corner of Park Lane and Queen Street used to be known as the Park Vaults. It used to be a real spit and sawdust pub with church seats!

A photograph from an advertisement for the 100-bedroom Angel Hotel.

The original Angel Hotel, which stood in Angel Street, dated to 1666. It moved to its present site in 1882.

The Cardiff Arms Hotel (1792–1878), from which the world famous Cardiff Arms Park took its name, was situated in Broad Street, a short thoroughfare which ran at right angles to both Castle Street and Angel Street.

The Royal Hotel in St Mary Street dates to around 1866. It underwent a multi-million pound refurbishment in 2001.

The Sandringham Hotel in St Mary Street was established in 1792 when it was known as the Black Lion. A stone lion can still be seen on the top of the building.

The Park Hotel in Queen Street, now a Thistle Hotel, was built in the French Renaissance style in 1885.

Many older Cardiffians will remember the Alexandra Hotel in Queen Street, formerly Crockherbtown, which was built in 1875.

The Queens Hotel in St Mary Street, left of picture, was established in around 1895 and was built on the site of the Pine Apple and Rock and Fountain.

The Theatre Royal in St Mary Street was known as the Talbot Arms between 1855–1910. It later became the offices of Brains Brewery. The Royal Hotel can be seen left of picture.

The Great Western Hotel established around 1876 was known as the Old Monk, but was renamed the Bush Pig in February 2004. It is now known as The Great Western.

The Duke of Wellington on The Hayes was established in 1892 and this picture was taken more than 100 years later. It is now known as Wellingtons.

The Albert, established in 1872, was rebuilt in 1910. It was closed for refurbishment in 2002 and reopened in 2003 as part of a multi-million pound luxury development of apartments and is now the Yard Bar and Kitchen.

The upstairs lounge in the Albert.

Known to generations of Cardiffians as the Blue Bell, this historic High Street pub was sadly renamed the Goat Major in 1995. It was established in 1813.

The Owain Glyndwr in Church Street was formerly the Buccaneer and before that the Tennis Court. The site was first occupied in 1731 by the Maply Arms.

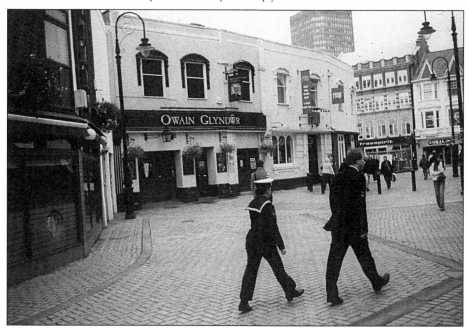

The Golden Cross on Hayes Bridge Road is a listed building. It opened in 1849 as the Shield and Newcastle Tavern and was renamed the Castle Inn in 1855. It became the Golden Cross in 1863.

Like the Golden Cross, the Kings Cross, established in 1872, is noted for its gay atmosphere.

Once known as the Cardiff Cottage, this St Mary Street pub, dating to 1863, is now The Cottage.

The Queen's Vaults in Westgate Street became the Flyhalf & Firkin in 1995. It has now reverted to its original name. It was well patronised by staff of the Western Mail & Echo offices which stood on the site of the building right of picture until they were demolished in 1963.

First licensed in 1847, the Salutation in Hayes Bridge Road stopped serving its customers in 1982.

The Lifeboat Tavern, formerly known as Lifeboat Inn, in Little Frederick Street, dated to 1897. It was demolished in 1978 to make way for a multi-storey car park. In the picture is the pub's last landlord, Ron Dowling.

Quay Street in 1891. Halfway up the street on the left of the picture once stood the Ship on Launch Arms, now known as the Model Inn.

This recent picture of the Model Inn was taken in the opposite direction to the one above. Compare the windows in this picture with the ones in the older picture.

The Horse & Groom in Womanby Street outlived the Red Cow, which had stood adjacent to it and which dated to 1776.

O'Neill's in Trinity Street was known as the Market Tavern and earlier still the Newmarket Tavern. It was established in 1909.

Previous page: The Cambrian in St Mary Street was built in 1830 and rebuilt in 1889. Known as Mulligans in the 1990s, it is now Kitty Flynn's.

The Old Arcade in Church Street was originally called the Arcade & Post Office and dated to 1844.

The Traders Tavern in David Street, formerly the Panorama, was built in the 1970s.

The Greyhound in Bridge Street shortly before it was demolished in 1981. It was established 1777.

The Queens Head in Bridge Street, established in 1858, can be seen right of picture. The Lord Palmerston, the Lion, Hope & Anchor, East Dock and the Nags Head were some of the other pubs situated in Bridge Street in days long gone.

This is how the City Arms in Quay Street looked in 1935.

International singing star Shirley Bassey once performed in the Cardiff Comrades Club and Institute in Paradise Place demolished around 1978.

An advertisement postcard for Raper's Temperance Hotel which stood on the corner of Westgate Street and Wood Street and was established in 1858.

Stevens & Son wine and spirit merchants in High Street, c.1903.

The date on the front of the York Hotel in East Canal Wharf is 1890. However, police report records date it to 1876.

Yates's in Westgate Street is situated on the site of the old Jackson Hall. Designed by George E. Robinson, it opened in 1878 and was originally the Cardiff Racquet & Fives Court.

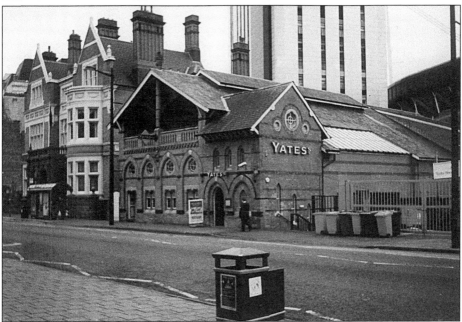

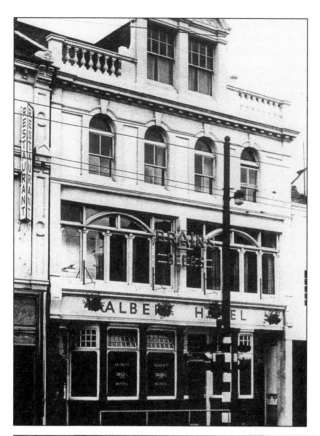

Left and below: The Albert Hotel in the 1950s. Unfortunately, the names of the two people in the bottom picture are unknown.

Fulton and Dunlops can be seen behind the gentlemen's toilets. The third building from the left of picture is the Rummer Tavern, or Hallinans as it was known when this picture was taken in the 1950s.

Bed and breakfast in the Terminus was just three shillings and sixpence in 1900. Known as Sam's Bar in the 1990s, it was renamed Zync in 2005.

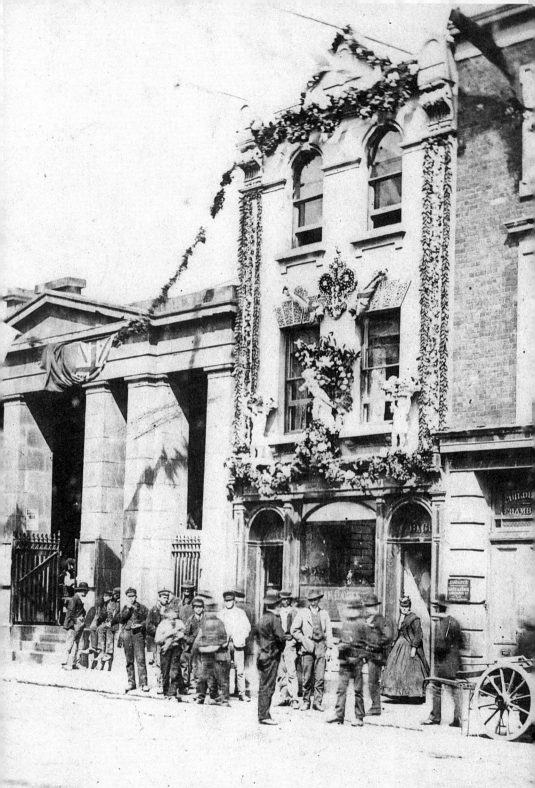

The Borough Arms in St Mary Street was decorated
for the wedding of the 3rd Marquis of Bute in 1872.

The Bute Arms, left of picture, was decorated for Queen Victoria's Silver Jubilee celebrations.

Chapter Two

CANTON, RIVERSIDE AND
A FEW OTHER PLACES

Established in 1883, the Cross Inn in Cowbridge Road East had a short life as pubs go, closing in 1924. It is now the HSBC bank.

The Royal Oak, Cowbridge Road East. This picture was taken during World War One and the pub closed shortly afterwards.

These two pictures, taken years apart, show the Admiral Napier in Cowbridge Road East, established 1886. The bottom picture was taken in 1960 when most of the Canton area was flooded.

The top picture shows how the Ty Pwll Coch Hotel in Cowbridge Road East looked before it was rebuilt in 1930 and the bottom one how it looked six years later.

These two pictures show how the Lamb & Flag on the corner of Picton Place and Cowbridge Road East has changed over the years.

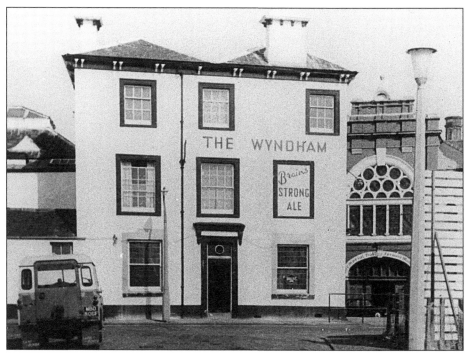

Established in 1881, the Wyndham Hotel in Canton originally had stables which could accommodate 12 horses. It is now used as offices.

Regulars of the Insole in Glamorgan Street posed for this picture in the 1920s.

The Insole as it is today. The pub is mentioned in Cardiff author Howard Spring's novel *Heaven Lies About Us*.

The Greyhound in Wellington Street, Canton, was established in 1897 and in 1988 was sold and converted into office accommodation.

Not long after this picture was taken the Ninian Park Hotel was demolished in 1978. Originally known as the Atlas Hotel, it had a change of name after Cardiff City AFC won promotion in the 1920s. A new Ninian Park Hotel was built on the site to the right of the picture.

Both these Wellington Street pubs, the Rover Vaults (above) and The Red Cow (below) were demolished many years ago. The former was built in around 1882 and the latter in around 1886.

Another Wellington Street pub was the Duke of York, which was established in 1887 and closed in 1975.

Freda Chinnick (centre), landlady of the Halfway, enjoying a drink with two of her regulars.

The offices and stores of Ind Coope Ltd on the Corner of Cowbridge Road and Radnor Road. The Maltings was built on the frontage of the building. Note the Double Diamond advertisement in the top picture.

A 1930s student rag parade travelling through Canton gives Brain's Brewery a good opportunity to advertise its beer.

A trade poster for the Ely Brewery Co. Ltd.

The Westgate, Cowbridge Road East. The old Westgate was demolished in the 1930s.

This large building, situated on the Taff Embankment, became the Inn on the River in 1974. It is due to be demolished to make way for a block of apartments.

This off-licence was situated in Wellington Street, Canton, *c.*1913.

Patrons of the King's Castle in Canton were given free bread and cheese. The pub was established 1889.

The Canton was formerly known as the Canton Cross Inn and was originally a coaching inn. From 1860 to 1904 it was the Canton Cross Brewery.

Another old Canton alehouse is the Foresters in Cowbridge Road East, established in 1882.

Members of Canton Liberal Club enjoying a game of cards, *c.*1920.

Forty years or so later and a card game is still popular with some members.

The old snooker room at the Canton Liberal Club, *c.*1920.

The 'new' snooker room, Canton Liberal Club, *c.*1960.

'Hold on while I straighten my tie!' Canton Liberal Club, c.1960.

Canton Liberal Club, c.1960.

Luther Jones (left) and Neil Brown force a smile for the photographer. Canton Liberal Club, 1961.

'Don't look now, but I think someone is taking our picture!' Canton Liberal Club, 1961.

These Canton Liberal Club members have no qualms about posing for the photographer.

Joe Link, secretary of Canton Liberal Club, is left of picture. Bert Jenkins, the treasurer, is to his right. The other members are Terry Paarl and Tony Gready, c.1978.

All hands to the pumps! Ken Connelly, Maureen Bunt and Joanne Piddel lend a helping hand.

Canton Liberal Club was awarded the King of Clubs award for the social club of the year in 2000.

Canton Liberal Club outing, August 1983.

Canton Liberal Club outing, c.1987.

The Halfway in Cathedral Road was originally known as the Halfway House. It has recently been refurbished and is haunted by 'an old man'. It was established 1889.

Another recently-refurbished pub is the Corporation Hotel in Canton, which was built on the site of a large farmhouse in 1889.

The Romilly in Romilly Crescent once had a club room over the stable. Established 1898.

Established in 1901, The Robin Hood in Severn Road is 244 yards from its nearest rival pub, the Romilly.

Don Ross (left) with Jack Clifford pulling pints in the Craddock Hotel in Ninian Park Road, *c.*1960.

Regulars of the now vanished York Hotel in East Canal Wharf were in a party mood on this pub outing in the 1950s.

Mr and Mrs Bill Chinnick, who kept the Halfway, and Mr and Mrs Tom Thomas, licencees of the Craddock, at a Cardiff Licensed Victuallers Association function at the Park Hotel, c.1970.

Another Cardiff Licensed Victuallers Association function at the Park Hotel, 1971. Extreme right of picture is the Bishop of Llandaff Eryl Stephen Thomas. Fourth from the right is Sir Charles Hallinan, who in 1975 became Lord Mayor of Cardiff.

These Cardiff landladies of the 1960s and 1970s also had their good times, as both these pictures illustrate.

Chapter Three

SOME SPECIAL OCCASIONS

Members of the Municipal Club, City Road, posed for this picture in The Parade before setting off on their annual club outing, *c.*1935.

Municipal Club members outing, *c.*1950.

Railway Club, Maindy Road. Left to right are Jean Newbury, Margaret Watts, Eunice Jolly, Jack Jolly and Beryl Harvey, c.1975.

These ladies of the Railway Club, Maindy Road, skittle club posed with their trophies for this picture, c.1970.

'We won the Cup!' Municipal Club members celebrate their darts championship win at the Flora Hotel in Cathays, c.1960.

On this occasion it was the Municipal Club's successful skittle team that were all smiles, c.1960.

Ray Impney (left) and his brother Terry show off the Cardiff Darts League Cup won by the Municipal Club, 1960.

Both these pictures were taken at the Comrades Club in Paradise Place.

Municipal Club members Ray Impney, Bobby Dewey and Bob Harding with the Rose Bowl Skittles Trophy, *c.*1950.

With their flagons of Brain's Mild much in evidence, these members of the Railway Club, Maindy Road, are about to set off on their annual club outing, *c.*1950.

Cathays Conservative Club on the corner of Wyeverne Road and Fitzroy Street. Members celebrated Queen Elizabeth's Coronation in 1953 by posing for this picture.

Cathays Conservative Club members Albert Parfitt, Bill Parfitt, Bill Duggan and Tommy Richards, c.1950.

Cathays Conservative Club members annual outing, c.1950.

These Cathays Conservative Club members are seen aboard a Campbell steamer heading for Weston-super-Mare, c.1955.

The Cardiff and District Licensed Victuallers' Association Ladies Auxiliary visited Arthur Guinness & Son's Park Royal Brewery on 24 January 1956.

Visit to the Park Royal Brewery by the Cardiff & District Licensed Victuallers' Association on 20 November 1959.

These two pictures show members of the Cardiff & District Licensed Victuallers' Association on the steps of the National Museum of Wales in Cathays Park before setting off on their annual outing, c.1960.

Visit to Park Royal Brewery by the Cardiff Licensed Victuallers' Association Ladies Auxiliary on 5 April 1965.

The AC/DC Civil Service Club skittle team which won the first mixed skittles league championship in 1980. The league was formed by Toni Jones (third from right, back row) who played alongside his wife Gillian.

Chapter Four

CATHAYS, ROATH AND ADAMSDOWN

In this picture Lily and Tommy Williams are serving drinks in the upstairs room of the Flora, *c.*1960.

Looking at the amount that has been rung up on the till, it appears that the price of a pint was 1s 3d when this picture was taken, 1961.

The top picture shows how the Woodville Hotel in Woodville Road looked in 1881 and the bottom picture how it looked a few years ago when the building was given a coat of yellow paint.

The Gower Hotel in Gwennyth Street dates to 1898 and has always been a popular pub with pigeon fanciers.

Built around 1891, the refurbished Crwys in Crwys Road is some 550 yards from the Gower Hotel.

The End, on the corner of Wyeverne Road and Coburn Street, was originally known as the Cockburn. After it was bombed during the last war and later rebuilt it was called the New Ely. Established 1882.

The Mackintosh in Mundy Place was named after the Mackintosh of Mackintosh who owned a lot of land in Cardiff. The pub was being refurbished when this picture was taken in September 2003. Established 1881.

The Cottage in Sanquahar Street dates to 1900, but this picture of it was taken in the 1970s. It was closed for refurbishment in the autumn of 2003.

Before they set off on a day trip, regulars of The Cottage and their children had this picture taken outside the pub, c.1930.

Workers of the Albany Box Company held their skittle presentation evenings in The Cottage during the 1950s.

Charlotte Chant (left), a barmaid at The Cottage, with John George and his mother Kitty who ran the pub.

Roasted salted peanuts were threepence a packet when John George was serving pints in The Cottage.

This picture, taken many years later, shows John George and his sister Pat Fishlock. The family ran the pub for more than 40 years.

The Roath Cottage on the corner of Plasnewydd Road and Rose Street dates to 1878. This picture of the Roath Cottage was taken in the 1930s and the portly gentleman in the doorway is licensee Mr Patten.

The Roath Cottage today.

The sign on the outside of the Claude in Albany Road tells us that it was built in 1890. It boasts a ten-pin bowling alley.

The Roath Park in City Road, formerly Castle Road, dates to 1886.

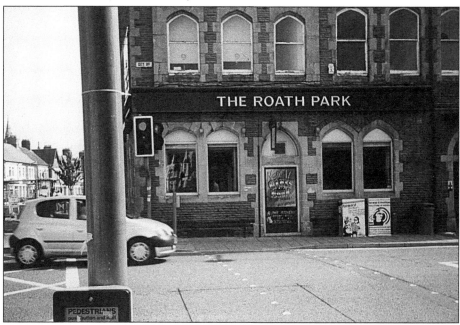

The Exchange in City Road had a 'Pub To Let' sign on it when this picture was taken in October 2003. It is now known as Cornerstones.

Just a matter of yards from The Exchange and still going strong is the Tut 'N' Shive, which was once known as the Ruperra. Established 1893.

The Royal Oak in Broadway had a boxing gym upstairs and the licensees at one time were relatives of Peerless Jim Driscoll. The pub used to be the headquarters of Roath (Cardiff) Harriers and in 1896 a meeting was held there which saw the formation of the Welsh Cross Country Association.

Established in 1887, the New Dock Tavern has been described as 'a working men's drinker, serving a good pint.'

Another Broadway pub is the Bertram Hotel, which dates to 1875.

With karaoke every Wednesday and a disco every Saturday regulars of the Locomotive were not short of entertainment.

A poltergeist haunts the cellar of The Clifton in Broadway. Established 1886.

The Crofts, formerly the Croft Hotel, in Croft Street, Roath. It was entirely rebuilt in 1958 after being bomb damaged during World War Two. It was established in 1881.

The Bar YK in Elm Street, Roath, was originally the Four Elms when it was established in 1890 and was known in the 1990s as the Yellow Kangaroo.

The White Swan in Shakespeare Street, Roath, was demolished in 1972. A feature of the pub was a large white swan painted on the roof. It was painted over in black during the last war for fear that it would be seen by Nazi bombers! Established 1879.

The Royal George on the corner of Crwys Road and Mackintosh Place is haunted by Humphrey, a friendly poltergeist. The pub was established in 1891.

Now known as an 'It's a Scream' pub, this building has also been known as Clancy's Irish Bar. When this picture was taken in 2001 it was called The George.

Tommy and Lily Williams (first and second left), landlord and landlady of the Flora Hotel, enjoying a drink with their customers, *c.*1970.

Mrs Sarah Driscoll of the Railway Club is presented with a skittles trophy.

At the time of his retirement, John Shergold, who managed the Three Arches in Llanishen, was the longest serving Brain's pub landlord in Britain. However, his wife Phyllis, who worked as a barmaid there before she married him, clocked up 32 years in the pub to John's almost quarter of a century.

The very popular Three Arches Hotel, which opened in time for the Queen's Coronation in 1953.

Members of Qualitex Print had their staff Christmas dinner at the Three Arches on 6 December 1960.

Landlord of The Three Arches John Shergold (centre) posed for this picture with the winners of a darts competition.

The author's wife, Jacqueline Lee, and Ron Humphries enjoy a joke in The Three Arches pub in 2002.

The same old crowd and the same old corner and it's standing room only again, 2002.

One of the first landlords of the Heath Hotel in Whitchurch Road when it opened in 1899 was John Applegate. The pub has been refurbished and extended over the years, but sadly the gargoyles, which used to be a feature in the lounge bar, have disappeared.

Chapter Five

MAINLY WHITCHURCH,

BIRCHGROVE AND LLANDAFF

The Birchgrove in Caerphilly Road dates back to the 1770s. Rebuilt in 1923, it was refurbished in 2001.

Just a matter of yards from the Birchgrove is the comparatively new New Inn.

The Three Horse Shoes in Merthyr Road replaced an old coaching inn which was demolished to make way for a new road. The pub has won awards for the 'Best Kept Cellar' and one year was voted 'Pub of the Year'.

Above and below: extended in 1962, the Plough in Merthyr Road is another popular pub.

These two pictures show the Maltsters Arms in Merthyr Road, another pub which has undergone great changes and improvements over the years.

Cardiff Rugby Club players Justin Thomas (left) and Jonathan Humphries (right) with the cheque which was presented to Velindre Hospital on behalf of the regulars of the Maltsters Arms, 1998.

Maltsters Arms, Whitchurch. The winners of a summer four-a-side skittle competition, 2001.

Charity pool competition, Maltsters Arms, *c.*1998.

Almost certainly the smallest pub in Whitchurch is the Royal Oak, which has catered for its patrons for more than a century.

The Fox and Hounds in Old Church Road, Whitchurch, was extended during the 1970s.

The Elms on Whitchurch Common was until quite recently known as the Three Elms. This former coaching inn is haunted. It is now The Three Elms once more.

Built on the site of a pub called the Red Cow is the Cow and Snuffers in Llandaff. Disraeli is said to have stayed there overnight.

The Black Lion, Cardiff Road, Llandaff, another old established inn.

One of the oldest pubs in Llandaff is the Maltsters Arms. This is another pub that is said to be haunted. It was rebuilt in the 1950s.

A well known haunt of rugby enthusiasts in 2000, the Butchers Arms in High Street, is close to Llandaff Cathedral.

The Heathcock in Bridge Street, Llandaff, 2000, was originally known as the Black Grouse.

Chapter Six

MAINLY DOCKLANDS, SPLOTT AND GRANGETOWN

The Ship and Pilot in James Street, established in 1861, was originally a coach house with stables. It was refurbished in 1994.

Nellie Collins was the last landlady of the Albion in Bute Street, which closed shortly after this picture was taken in 1906.

Inside the Albion Hotel, 1906.

A favourite pub with the ladies of the night was the Custom House in Bute Street. Opened in around 1859, it was demolished in the late 1990s.

Sydney Peel was landlord of the White Hart Inn in James Street when this picture was taken.
The pub dates to 1855 and the nearest pub to it was the Stag's Head.

Another long gone docklands pub is the North and South Wales in Louisa Street, established in 1892.

A recent picture of the Packet Hotel in Bute Street, which is popular with office workers. Established 1864.

The West Dock, which used to be in Herbert Street, was established in 1865. Englands, the potato merchants warehouse, can be seen in the background.

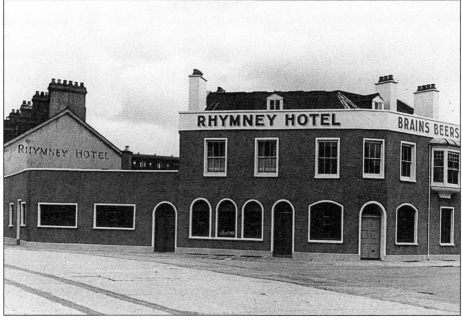

The Rhymney Hotel in Adam Street was established in 1858. Rumples was built on the site in the 1990s.

The Bute Dock Hotel in West Bute Street dates to 1839, the year the Bute West Dock was opened.

Little did John Smith (right, back row) think when this picture was taken in the New Sea Lock Hotel in 1955 that one day he would become Lord Mayor of Cardiff. Others in the picture are Nicky Payne, Jacky Peters, Don Salter and Graham Nicholas.

The Adamsdown Hotel darts team which won the Lord Mayor's four-a-side Tournament 1966–7. Left to right are Jack Powell, John Sennett, Danny Shanaghan, Billy Holden, Doug Fox (captain), Charlie Ford and Jimmy Ford.

The Splottlands Hotel, Meteor Street, established in around 1883, was at one time known as the Splott Inn. The name of the ghost who haunts this pub is Matilda.

The Neville Hotel in Clare Road, being close to Ninian Park Football Ground and the Welsh White City Stadium at Sloper Road, was a great favourite with soccer and greyhound racing fans before the last war. Established 1889.

This Ferry Road pub was originally known as the Railway Hotel and later the Penarth Railway Hotel. However, since 1926 it has been the Red House and in 2003 plans were being made, against strong opposition, to demolish it to make way for a housing complex.

This picture of the Cornish Mount in Patrick Street was taken shortly before it was demolished in 1967. Mrs Clare Smith was the last landlady. Established 1855.

The Moorland Hotel in Moorlands Road was haunted by a former landlord, Mr Pugh, who hanged himself around 70 years ago. The hotel is now closed.

Chapter Seven

AROUND AND ABOUT

The Hollybush in Pentwyn was opened in 1977. There is a much older Hollybush in Corytown.

The Bulldog Inn in Pentrebane Road, Fairwater, was opened in 1965.

The Discovery in Celyn Avenue, Lakeside, was named after one of Captain Scott's ships which sailed to the Antarctic.

One of Cardiff's newest pubs is the Allensbank or Brewsters, as it is now called, in Wedal Road.

An early picture of the historic Blue Bell Inn, Newport Road, St Mellons.

This is how the Rompney Castle in Wentloog Road, Rumney, looked after it was renovated in 1932.

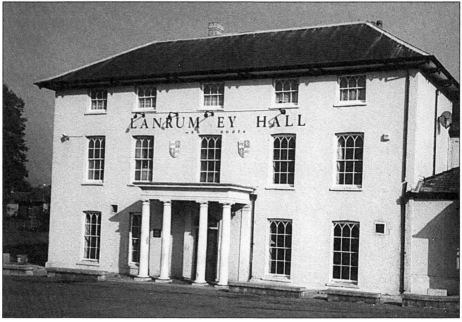

It was from the former stately home Llanrumney Hall that the first point-to-point steeplechase in Wales took place in 1896.

One of Cardiff's oldest pubs is the Carpenter's Arms in Newport Road, Rumney.

The White Hart in Tyr Winch Road, St Mellons.

Another old pub in St Mellons is the Unicorn. In days long gone the Swansea to London coach used to stop there.

The Star Inn, St Mellons, is a listed building and once boasted four darts teams!

The Old Cross Inn, Newport Road, is a great favourite with locals.

The gentleman directly behind the skittler is Bill Chinnick landlord of
the Halfway, Cathedral Road, *c.*1963.

Bibliography

Cardiff Yesterday series, various volumes, Stewart Williams.

The Cardiff Book, Stewart Williams.

The Complete Guide to Cardiff's Pubs 1995 & 1996, David Matthews.

Records of the County Borough of Cardiff.

Report on Licensed Premises 1903 & 1906, compiled by Graham Williams.

Historic Inns of Cardiff by Alan J. Harbidge, 1986 (unpublished).

The Pub-Goers Guide Book, A select guide to the pubs of Cardiff.

The Western Mail, South Wales Echo, South Wales Daily News, Evening Express, Cardiff Times, Cardiff and Suburban News, Cardiff Independent.

ND - #0324 - 270225 - C0 - 234/156/10 - PB - 9781780911816 - Gloss Lamination